Words in My Head

LOVE, SEX, SADNESS AND MADNESS

www.AyodejiOtuyelu.com

Words in my Head

Copyright ©2020 by Ayodeji Otuyelu
The year of Covid-19

All rights reserved. This book or any portion thereof may not be reproduced or used in any manner whatsoever without the express written permission of the publisher except for the use of brief quotations in a book review.

Editors
Adewale Olowu
Biodun Abudu
Curu Necos-Bloice
Thabiso Mohohlo

Artwork
Benjamin Goetz

ISBN-13: 978-1-7352541-0-4

dedicated to all the beautiful souls waiting
to express the
words in their head.

my name is ayodeji! it means "doubled joy".
most of the time i wonder if i bring enough joy to the
life of those that named me. these words made me
realize that in order to bring joy to others,
i must fill my life with enough ayo (joy).

dEJI

CONTENTS IN MY HEAD

OUTLANDISH CHILD 1

LANA DEL REY 2

UNGODLY FEELING 4

NARCISSIST LOVER 5

THE DEVIL CRIES TOO 7

DEE-HELL 8

ADULTERER 10

FINDING EQUILIBRIUM 11

COLOGNE 12

TRAPPED IN MY SKULL 13

UN-HEALED 14

IROKO OLUWERE 16

CLOSED BOX 17

RELIGIOUSLY SHRUNK 18

UNFORGETTABLE PICTURE 19

- **MY VOW** 20
- **MENTALLY WEDGED** 21
- **OGOGORO REACTION** 22
- **YOU AND I** 24
- **THANK YOU, NEXT.** 26
- **WOMEN THAT KILL** 27
- **MAMA AGBA** 28
- **OLD ME** 30
- **DOUBLE EDGES** 32
- **NEW TESTAMENT** 33
- **STRENGTH OF A WOMAN** 34
- **LOVE MAGNET** 36
- **OCEAN OF SADNESS** 37
- **ESCAPE** 38
- **RACE ROULETTE** 39
- **CONVERSATION AT THE BAR** 41
- **SEE THROUGH ME** 42

- **THE BEAUTIFUL PAINT** 43
- **SCALDED HEART** 44
- **STILL DON'T KNOW WHAT LOVE IS** 45
- **19 YOUNG, BROKE AND FABULOUS** 46
- **THE SPACE BETWEEN US** 47
- **TOUCH ME DEEPLY** 48
- **SUMMER DALLIANCE** 49
- **LET GOD** 50
- **NEW YORK CITY** 51
- **YOU LOST ME** 53
- **INSOMNIA** 54
- **WALL OF JERICHO** 56
- **HOW MUCH MORE** 57
- **WHAT YOU SEEK** 58
- **DON'T CRY** 59
- **DEAR KAREN** 61
- **EXPOSED BY REALITY** 62

- THAT KIND OF LOVE
- LETTER TO MY EX
- UNREADY
- MOMENT THROUGH MY WINDOW
- MOTHERS
- CATATONIA
- UNWRITTEN MASTERPIECE
- OPPOSITES
- TAKING CHANCE
- CURSED CHILD
- TIED BY YOUR STRING
- MESSED UP LIKE ME
- THE NEXT STOP IS...
- LOOKING FOR AN ESCAPE
- HAIRITAGE
- CHOKE YOUR LOVER
- IMMIGRATION

ONE HIT WONDER 83

NOT AN ANGEL 84

FALLOW 85

CONVERSATION WITH SELF 86

LITTLE FIRES 87

LIKE A FRUIT 88

CHOICES 89

MY MASK 90

WHEN IS LOVE ENOUGH? 92

THE WHISPERER 93

TRAVELER 95

GRATEFUL 96

SOMEONE ELSE 97

CRAZY NANCY 98

JẸ-JẸ 99

LOOK AT YOU NOW 100

DIFFERENT WORLD 101

- [COVALENT BOND .... 102](#)
- [OUR FOOLISH PRIDE .... 103](#)
- [OBSESSION .... 104](#)
- [PRICELESS IMMORTALITY .... 105](#)
- [BLEEDING ROSE .... 106](#)
- [MY GUIDANCE .... 107](#)
- [FILTHY AND GUILTY .... 108](#)
- [UNPROTECTED SEX .... 109](#)
- [READY TO BE TAKEN .... 110](#)
- [I CAN'T BREATHE .... 111](#)
- [MY DOG AND I .... 113](#)
- [HUNTING .... 115](#)
- [EVERYTHING IN BETWEEN .... 118](#)
- [A WOMAN'S RELIGION .... 119](#)
- [GLOSSARY .... 122](#)

Thank you for supporting

Words in My Head

I hope it speaks to you

and ignites your innermost thoughts.

Feel free to write to me at

info@ayodejiotuyelu.com

Words in My Head

LOVE, SEX, SADNESS AND MADNESS

AYODEJI OTUYELU

Words in My Head   Ayodeji Otuyelu

outlandish child

she asked him many times to come home
from her voice one could tell she missed her outlandish son
the one that perfectly wore her make-up in secret
and silently admired other males on the street
she saw it all, but kept it hush-hush
he sighed and said, what will i come for, maami
it's a cold country with cold hearted people
why can't you just get an education and come home? she pleaded
maami, i love it here and i love the winter boots and jackets
i can be myself and be free without father's toxic male expectations

but here she is, in new york city on a winter day
struggling to identify the remains of her son in a mortuary
he was shot! she was shot by a transphobic american
she cries wondering if she is truly free now
her favorite outlandish son

lana del rey

god damn, son of a sinner woman

i missed the way we used to play cards

naked in your room and getting high

running around wildling like we were young bloods

bar hopping and making out in public bathrooms

people on the line smirking at us

my cum stuck on your beard and we laughed out loud

i yelled slut! then you went ahead and wrote a song about it

you loved and understood my accent so well

but with her, i always have to repeat myself

she doesn't like alternative music like you do

and she thinks lana del rey is too sad and depressing

while with you, we listened from born to die to norman fucking rockwell

drinking and pretending we had it all,

above all, we had nothing

not the best but it was the best for us

god bless us sons of sinner women

i miss you and i hope one day she dies, and maybe i'd find my way back to you

and if death takes me before her

publicize all we did behind closed doors at my funeral

ungodly feeling

we sat together under the hot nigerian sun

drinking palm wine and smoking weed

we laughed out so loud and free

looking me, looking you,

eye to eye

you sipped from the calabash and so did i

our legs gently touched and we both smiled

we both understood that forbidden fruit we craved

but i didn't want to be eve, neither did you

gently we let the emotions burn-out like the wrap in our fingers

as the girls joined and the conversation changed

time never stood still, but that feeling

that ungodly feeling

remains the same

narcissist lover

always making it all about you
still i don't mind, i just let it slide
the fire in you is sure from hell
burning bridges and slowly killing
no one treats me the way you do
it hurts, but i must find a way to cope with you

don't tell me to work on my self esteem
you don't listen nor pay attention
i love you still and i think you love me too
but i'm at the background fanning your embers
and you act like you don't see me
you forget that i'm still here
looking for how to cope with you

they said i've given away all my joy
i feel like a walking cadaver
i need to leave and live without you
but how do i live without you?
i'm getting tired of settling in this shadow
still finding ways to cope without you.

the devil cries too

i've got troubles of my own, glued to my skin
they keep my tears streaming down my cheek
then i pour myself a cheap glass of red wine
and shout hallelujah to the almighty and divine
i can drink something so cheap and less fine
but its sure taste good in my lonely abyss

they all like to think i am alive and happy
i did a great job hiding the coffin in my soul
it drains me every day because it's so heavy
who cares! roll out of bed into the pretense
sing a joyful song and cheers to more fun
it's not that fun, it's just another act

dee-hell

sometimes

i feel that rush like a winter rain

cold in me,

running in my veins and i freeze

but then

you're gone

i feel so heated and empty,

furnaced by you

must have been a hundred and ten degrees

i want to scream!

but it hammers my head and

i just lay there not sure if i'm going to love or die

you told me how much you love me, yet you go out there

to use the same mouth to eat a pussy,

i'm sure it's juicy

what do you really want man?

my beautiful dl

i am not an angel

and i never pretended to be one

because i love you with my wildness

but you begged me to stay tamed

and unleashed my demons only in the bedroom

that's when you are proud of me

and yet you chose to see me

like a being specially thrown to this earth by the hands of grace,

fuck it! that's rough

if you can't be man enough to own it like it's yours

that's on you baby,

i'm done putting my emotions in your limbo

you shoot me high like dope and leave me wondering,

shit, it puts my brain on pause

and this whole dl thing is lumpy

i have been hiding way too long

and i am just done.

adulterer

i know he loves his wife

he talked about her and his eyes ignited

but the undeniable joy he got when he laid in my bed

passes all understanding

he looked at the time and joked about how it runs like hares

everyone else saw him for who he really was and judged him so hard

but i just let him lay there so he could hide away and laugh

i know he will never leave his wife

sometimes he wished it was easy, but life is always hard

i was aware of what we will never be, but he loved what we were

he pretended we would be together forever,

but he put on his shoes and kissed me goodbye

it was time to disappear

he warned me to keep my feelings for him at bay

finding equilibrium

pivoted at the center of it all
trying to strike a balance between everything and more
the rock-hard toll is dribbling on my happiness
my family, friends and who i want to be
my father doesn't seem to be the best to look up to
running could launch me into the goal i desire
but my decisions emanated with loneliness
silly of me to think i can do it all by myself and be sane
picking up my pieces knowing i will sacrifice so much
for the little i am asking for, in this large life

cologne

i still wrestle myself the way you fought me
this time i am doing it all alone without you
your whispers still wake me up from sleep
but i never catch a word of what you said
i could swear you are in this room everyday
or maybe
i deceived myself with your cologne that i sprayed

trapped in my skull

always looking to disappear
but every morning i find myself here
in this dark nut-space called my head
screaming but no one can hear
stuck in a loop maybe i should shoot
running in the cycle of my own axis is exhausting
no windows, no doors, just my skull.

un-healed

remember the cold summer

all coated up in my emotions and sadness

black coat, black pants and runny nose

my clarks boot making its way through the dirty slushy earth

my glass heart was broken in fall

winter intensified the ache in my chest

cried all day and night and ended up with a fever

summer finally came, but i couldn't enjoy the heat

i let the sunshine dry up my wound

let go of the coat of sadness

but couldn't trust the compliments from strangers

when i exposed my skin

all i see are scars from the past

too blind to see them beautifying my back

actually, it's all trapped in my feelings

scarred, wounded and scratched

but yet i wish for a new day with happiness and kisses

it's fall again and i wonder what happened during summer

maybe i healed, i healed

will i fall again, this coming fall?

iroko oluwere

she is not a flower please!
she is a tree!
she doesn't stay still to bloom in the morning
for you to smell or beautify yourself
nor does she wait to be watered and adored by your eyes
she is rooted into the crust of the earth
and with branches strong enough to keep you from falling
yet she produces sweet fruits standing tall with her head high
she is not just a woman
more than a wife
she creates with her two hands
and yet can destroy, if you stand in her way

closed box

i let them define me by their standards of beauty
i keyed into these figures, but i was found wanting
definitely not this hair
the huge rubber like lips of mine
they just don't fit into the box
but do you know what else is boxed?
a dead man!

religiously shrunk

the saddest part is hiding

hiding the best part of me from them

my loved ones

they only see a fragment of me

i shrank to their comfort

twisted to what i believed will make them happy

finding my own happiness is dependent

i must lose or gain

happiness and freedom are not for sale

gaining new friends who over the years turned into family

and losing family who yanked me off

because of their beliefs and religion

god bless us all

i wonder who they are protecting

myself or their ego

i know for sure, jesus needs not their protection

unforgettable picture

clumsy with a sound
flaccid with a look
sick and weak every week
but yet i still think of you

hopeless in the head
helpless in the bed
sick and weak every day
but yet i won't leave

lifeless without a glow
disease took your soul
as we plant your remains
memory of your seamless face stays.

my vow

death will come

if i do good or bad

but i chose to be good with my life

i will age

if i stay or leave

but i chose to grow old with you

time won't stop

if i love or hate

but i chose to spend my time loving you

mentally wedged

i can't live without you

and yet

i feel smothered when i'm with you

ogogoro reaction

just like alcohol
one minute you feel so high
expressive and motivated
you keep it going
gulping it down your throat
sometimes your palate resist
but your brain says, you can do it

just like alcohol
another minute you feel so sad
bad ass hangover and you regret every sip
feeling half dead with headaches
and some people get a liver break
addiction takes you to an aa meeting
or you get arrested for dui

just like alcohol

we will do it again

some cowards will shy off

some will just play safe

whatever way you play the game

what makes you safe can expose you

and what exposes you can keep you safe.

you and i

you and i
will catch a falling star
will stand the test of time
and love where the leaf is greener

you and i
will travel the world side by side
do crazy things of life and get wild
like we are animals in the jungle

but you and i
couldn't wait for a star to fall
we broke and failed the test of time
and we never see a leaf get greener

you and i

travelled on the separate sides of life

got crazy, wild and broke apart

we are truly like careless animals

and we forgot who we really are

no more you, no more i

thank you, next.

to all the hands that fed me

to all the arms that held me

to all the eyes that beheld my beauty

and to all the tongues that made me feel guilty

thank you.

women that kill

straight into his heart
she plunged the knife
twisted it hard twice
he screamed and fell to the ground

his blood painted her crimson
she smelled it and it felt so good
she cut through his life ribbon
and saw his life leave so soon

on the floor, so frigid and soaked
she knew he was dead, but she didn't care
picked up the keys and drove away
she sent her husband to hell and hoped to see him there

mama agba

my grandmother, strong and full of grace
for whatever reason, i was the apple of her eyes
that's what she said when no one was around
i loved to listen to the tales of her childhood
her voyage to becoming the woman she was and before
her long travels, the make-up and how she beat up the boys
she was one of a kind in sapele

one day, during our late night kokoro
sitting on her bed while playing with her tiny dry toes
in her 80s, she surprisingly fought a stroke and came back to life
i asked her "mama, what was your first experience like"
she closed her eyes and waved her hand in the air
that's her way of dismissing a question
but she knows i am as stubborn as my grandfather
she understood i wouldn't let it rest until she let the cat out
"why do you want to know what my first experience was like?"
i replied "because i am always curious about the women in my life"
i noticed stagnant tears

more like pain, regret and a few drops of happiness
fighting to hold it back, but her eyes remained soaked
she grinned and said in a soft tone
"i was only with two men all my life
the one that broke my pot before i got to the stream
and the one that fixed my pot and watered-a-new flower out of me"

with so many questions in my head,
i knew i would be kicked out of her room
i have never seen her so sober and still
looking like an angel but also vulnerable
with all the confidence in me i asked again
gently rubbing more shea butter on her feet
mama! why didn't you protect your pot?
tears rolled out as she winced
i tried but i was 10! and he was in his 40's
she turned her face to the wall and told me to turn the light off
we never talked about it again
my grandmother, beautiful resilient human
full of grace, i pray she finds rest in her grave

old me

i remember this face

in that small old place

you were young, full of life and sneaky

you told yourself

you do not belong here

you ran everywhere looking for love and some quickies

so far, you've got away

to a cold lonely place

you bought yourself so much and some more

but love felt so far away like home

you settled for peace and freedom

or maybe it's just another lie to keep yourself away

i surely remember you well
you're what i used to be twenty years ago
everything that i wanted when i was ten
now i think back
with what i know now
wishing to turn back the hand of time
and maybe make some corrections

double edges

from the genesis

i knew this love tree would yield no fruits

but i chose to find beauty in the dried leaves

i watered it

i nurtured it

every morning, i prayed for the sun to shine bright

yet, the tree stunted and lost all its leaves

thought spring would make it better

or maybe summer would bring some magic

but it got worse with feeble branches

right in front of us it withered

even if we don't cut this tree now

it's going to dry up and die by itself

won't waste my time burning it down

no wood from that tree will ever make a good fire

we knew before the revelation

we are not meant to be.

new testament

one day,

i will be done with everything that did not bring me peace,

bit by bit

i will remove everything that reduces me to shit

may take days

but i will sweep every nook and cranny of my mind and soul

and discard everything that did not glorify my existence

like a warrior

with sword and arrows, i will break every shackle

holding me back from actualizing myself

and purge out all glue holding my tongue

from saying the words in my heart

like a bird sing

i will speak out unafraid of who and what i will lose

but free myself from that mental cage i am in,

like a tractor

i will destroy everything and everyone that stands in my way,

including you!

strength of a woman

she used to be slim and smart
until i lived in her for nine months
she went through different stages
with me stretching her womb
dreamt of me before she met me
i didn't care, i was just in a warm safe place
i bet i didn't want to come out

knowing her breast won't be the same
she squeezed the food of life in my mouth
i sucked on it whenever i wanted to, disrespectfully
she didn't deny me the nutrients i needed to grow
i cried out loud, she became sober
i was numb she wondered and worried
i stared at her and enjoyed all the love she offered
and nothing else mattered to her,
but the selfish me who just wanted what i wanted regardless

she fought and won my unknown battle
yet she kept up with my selfish father who thought i'm taking all her time
in her weakness and strength
who complimented her for all she does?

why do they question the strength of a woman?
the power of the woman who carried and raised me to be who i am
her back is strong, and her smile lights the darkness that crawled in
and even though she broke down and cried sometimes
she stood up and pushed again
that was my younger sister
the joy and pain of motherhood.

love magnet

your x-ray eyes see through me

through the skeleton of my pain, lies and guilt

like a cheetah, i flee from your open arms

i am not afraid to call you my home

i'm only trying to save you from myself

your voice magnetizes me back to your presence

and your touch stills me to sub-zero

frozen in love with you, please don't make me melt.

ocean of sadness

you dug deep into the earth of my heart
the flood of my pain soaked your happiness
neither you nor i find peace of mind
if only you could return me to my darkness
maybe your super sun would rise again.

escape

the fear of dreaming without you next to me
and the peace in the reality of sleeping far from your body
it was a see-saw tale of the furious you and i
designed with a constant pain in form of god
and i worshipped every moment like a lunatic
sacrificing my blood pressure at your altar
waiting for you to drain all of me
so, i could have the strength to jet out of your life

and yes! you did, you left me with nothing
the least you could have done was disappear with the hate you gave
you swept my joy away, but i got a chance to be human again
each day i live missing your chaotic breeze
and every single mile away from your soul
keeps me stronger with a pinch of hope
if i love again or not
i will die knowing i finally put myself first.

race roulette

you got a gun
and a bullet
pull the trigger
and you become a killer
don't let their words decide for you
make up your mind on what to do
you want to shoot
or act a fool?

don't stand and cry
watch it rain in my eyes
you can end my life now
my soul will be lifted high
no gain without pain
but what will you gain?

aim to kill
shoot it please
make it quick
oh! my sorrow freezes
i don't need you to pity me
do it like a king
feed your pride with my blood!

don't stand and cry
watch it rain in my eyes
you can end my life now
my soul will be lifted high
no gain without pain
but what will you gain?

if you miss
you'll earn a goodbye kiss
but if you hit
i'll be gone, done, gone!
but you will live
to be shot someday soon
guess by who?

conversation at the bar

i said to him

i was told i'm the black sheep in the family

he looked at me

smiled and replied, so am i

i looked at him

frowned and replied but you're white

you should be the white sheep in your family

if he is the black sheep, then i am the white sheep

grammatical error or every negativity is just made black?

see through me

this is a song written out of pain

yes! just pain, not anger

pain of not being what i want to be

pain of not being able to love who i want to love

pain of not coming out but lying constantly about what i desire

i've lost my pretty smile, says my mirror

i could stare at the waves of wrinkles on my forehead

hiss and think of those good timeworn days

when this old man was a boy

not just a boy but a beautiful boy

i was so in love with myself and life

pregnant with big dreams and hopes to bring to life

then the older i got,

i realized i may live in this outfit till the day i die

that was my pain, this is my agony

like a winter tree, i want people to see what i have become.

the beautiful paint

perfection in his eyes
magnifico in his mind
he could feel his touch like a gentle breeze
but could not catch or give it a kiss

he could have brought him to life
but he is too shy to give it a try
maybe he is better as paint in his head
for he will be of no good in his bed

shy of meeting a shy painting he created
imprisoned by his oil and canvas
priceless monument of his fantasy
but it will never grace his reality

scalded heart

my scalded heart didn't heal
from the hurt and burn of my past
neither did my tears stop dripping
but over time, they froze-still
and i became so numb and cold
wickedness is as beautiful as glaciers.

still don't know what love is

stars made me black and blue
and my remains were abused and used
forgive me darling, i'm not easy to love
for i still don't know what love is.

19 young, broke and fabulous

your love for me won't foot the bills

stop telling me how you feel

i am young, broke and fabulous.

the space between us

underneath the dark sky
two hearts far apart
different ways but same thoughts
just want to be close to you my love

underneath the blue sky
two hearts asking why
different questions but same answer
i can't stand the distance any longer

days are short when we are together
nights are long cause you're miles farther
different worlds but same hunger
you're all that i want

touch me deeply

forget the shape of the earth
and look deep into my heart
do i make you feel so high?
or you're just teasing me with your lies

am i so beautiful on the outside?
or you can see through my inside
i'm alone and always lonely
waiting for someone, who will never be mine.

so many thoughts in my big head
make me keep rolling on my flat bed
as the breeze caresses me gently
i pray you touch my soul deeply

summer dalliance

this came from a place that hurts
more than getting burnt
this flows from a broken heart
moving on will be hard

i watched the sun rise in your face
and it set to darkness in quick pace
we danced and laughed to the stars
went separate ways before the moon

let god

they don't understand us
so, they said we are crazy
they said we are under a curse
that's why we won't make it
don't let their description describe us
won't let their words divide us

from father adam we've been cursed
the snake and fruit in the garden
god created them both
impure and insane
love conquers all
let god be the judge

new york city

the wonder of the high rise
as tall as the eiffel tower
beautify with thousands of city lights
who can deny the dream?
in new york city

it's hard to find a true love
but you sure can find great food
the fashionable people walking fifth avenue
and the beautiful people in harlem
welcome to new york city

big city, big life, big problems
this city can house you or make you homeless
with a bed of dreams bigger than jupiter
that's why the streets never sleep nor slumber
this is new york city

this is where the pieces of the whole world are boxed
don't let it swallow you, dream on
if you can make it here you can conquer anywhere
even if you don't make it here, there is hope somewhere else
you are in the city called new york.

you lost me

i waited half-way
and i have nothing to say
you never tried to meet me halfway
so, i called it a day

i lost you yesterday
but you didn't know until today
if only you freed yourself earlier
you and i would be together in may

i'm not going to stay
i don't care what price we pay
let's put this boat at bay
ahead is a new sun ray

insomnia

passed my bedtime
but my soul can't find rest
my bed peace left with day
even few glasses of wine
won't put me in a trance
a baton marathon in my heart
thumps like it's going to open my chest
the ringing church bell in my head
catalyze my temperature
i'm perplexed, lost and unsure
my prescription can't find me
it's 2:45 in the morning
i say to myself, this is new york
i don't need to be sleeping
it's a friday night
i need to go hang out
then i realize i ran out of friends few days ago
i have no lover and the only love i knew was from my mama
the rest are leftovers from an abusive relationship
i have always found comfort in my home

here i don't feel ashamed or afraid

but tonight, my home denies me security

it is suddenly a house to keep me out of december weather

my bed and comforter can't save me tonight

not even a prayer will calm my beating heart

this is a war i lose every night

wall of jericho

sometimes, the all i could lean on

are the demons that dwell inside of me

they get me through those days

when good can't push down my jericho walls.

how much more

how many more scars before my heart will rest?

how many more years before my eyes will dry?

how much more pain before i can feel the joy?

how many more men before i can find the one?

what you seek

money is not everything

but it could buy you some comfort in your anguish

love sometimes is never enough

but it might just be the happiness that you totally seek.

don't cry

if i die today before tomorrow
in a land totally unknown
let it be hell! let it be heaven
don't cry over my demise

remember i was full of love
just that my time was a quickie
i live my life the way i want
no questions asked. it's over now
please don't cry for my attention

i may not have millions
but i was truly loved
i may not have mansions
but you gave me a home when i needed it
just don't cry for my new home

remember time still ticks

and no one is shielded

drink my favorite liquor

and dance to my favorite song

no tears just laugh at my lifeless body.

dear karen

dear karen,

i am just as scared of you

as you are of me

we are all born the same way

from a woman

all will die at the end of the day

like every human.

exposed by reality

reality ripped the lies i wore like a garment
running down my face are the tears of regret
the pain strikes me back and forth and i groan
oh! i realize, when it's totally done and gone

it was all a hideaway that kept me thinking i'm better,
a pretense that made me feel like human
i thought everyone did it too, to stay one inch ahead
couldn't give it meaning nor make sense of it

the perfect walls of illusion i built around me
tumbled down exposing me to my fears
the true me appeared, shy, feeble and humbled
the only thing to lean on is the truth of what i became

that kind of love

sometimes he puts it down

soft and sweet

and sometimes he puts it down

hard and sour

i'm easy to touch

and he is hard to love.

letter to my ex

it's strange that i fall apart whenever you cross my mind
that's when i misplace the strength to hold back my tears
i scream your name knowing you are deaf to me now
i broke your heart and you shattered the illusion of a wonderful life
so many words could have been swallowed
and so many words i wish i'd vomited
if only i could format my memory storage of you
in despair, i'm fully aware it's not me you need
i hope in lonely night you recall you've lost me.

unready

everything was real
the kiss, the touch, even the fight

every emotion like a stream
yet deep, runs through you and i

we can't be tamed
our madness, our wants, our lust for life

we never lost it, ever!
we are just not ready to give up the sky.

moment through my window

like a lonely house
quiet, scared, and still
like a winter tree
dry with no leaves or fruits

like wounded skin
ugly, scarred and rough
like a war knight
strong, tough and ready to kill

the only peace within me
was found in solitude
but all i did was scream
because my wounds never healed

standing alone like a winter tree
every day is like a war
and i'm ready to kill
staring out of the window, unhealed

mothers

i can only photograph what it feels like to be a mother
demanding so much sacrifice and some wahala (trouble)
i look at my mother lifting the weight on her shoulders
and yet she loved, smiled and took it all

how did she wake up every morning before the cock crowed?
unloaded herself of my father's recklessness with other women
in pain and struggle, she saw me through school
and yet people call women a weak vessel

i saw her break into tears many times in her bedroom
then she sighs and walks to the kitchen to make us dinner
great food, from a great woman to nourish my soul
i wonder how she found a balance between being a wife,
a mother and her own career

i celebrate that resilient woman who sacrificed so much for that child
now my sister complains about motherhood and the branches that hang
i celebrate my unknown partner for the lot that comes with me
and my unborn child
i wish mothers genuine happiness, for all the great seeds they sow.

catatonia

experienced a fragment of death in flashes
i could feel the heat from hell, it burns
i skimmed through the antithesis of my life
back to consciousness from brief catatonia
i should do better
for those who love me

unwritten masterpiece

if it's not magical
or intensely soulful
if it doesn't make you bite your lips
i don't think you are making love
maybe you're just making babies

if it doesn't make you let go
or make you feel whole
if it doesn't make you feel erotically artistic
i think you are just horny
and looking for the next hole to ejaculate

sex is an art, defined in unusual ways
an unwritten masterpiece
you are the painter and the paint
you're the master and the slave
climax, pleasure burnt you to ashes like pompeii
your escape is the ink in form of unleashed fluid
splatter, it's a wonderful work of art.

opposites

heaven!

hell!

are you sure about it mama?

or you also learnt it from your mother?

black

white

why is my skin not named white?

i don't see in the bible where god named mine black

man

woman

if they are not equal

why did you go through the same pain giving birth to me and my sister?

taking chance

clamp my hands

and dance wild like david

for we don't know when we might be deaf to the music.

cursed child

i am the cursed child

i questioned the statutes of the society

i am the rebel that repudiated religion

even in the pool of fear i spoke my mind

i do not associate with tepid, must be hot or cold

in the presence of light, i challenged evil

love is love; all men are equal, gasped!

tell that to the scars on the backs of my ancestors

empowered by the melanin i carry

the beautiful poison to your soul.

tied by your string

i got drunk on the whiskey of your love

and i woke up with an abysmal hangover

gagging on the lies i swallowed through your kisses

if only i did not ingest your fluid

toxic to my sense of reasoning

but not a single regret

my head is finally clear

i can't release myself from your barrel

messed up like me

i can see you're pretty and messed up like me
we don't need light to shine, we glow in the dark
rough on the edges but smooth when we align
we are not ugly, we are just chaotically beautiful
engulfed by the cloud, rebirth in our torrent

the next stop is…

on the train to an unknown place
surrounded by strange sad faces
every stop screams torture from hell
is it me or we're all going through this phase?
this town can paint your innocence with pain
over time you model your pain with disdain

looking for an escape

i remember how i got here

it was through a stranger that preyed on my pain

i don't know how to get out of here

my therapist said through hard work and some grace

i know you've been trying to figure out the words i refused to say

honestly, i am just looking for an escape out of this cage

hairitage

my hair

my skin

my lip

my nose

constantly criticized because i am different

my overwhelming beauty you portrayed as ugly

through the lens of my mother and ancestors

i look into my image and i am well made

looking so strong with my back against all odds

does my confidence scare you?

my naturally full luscious lips

and the stream of melanin irradiating on my skin

you named black

and in your dictionary black stands for evil, death and sadness

black is the color of my beauty

the strength and elegance infused in my blackness

the versatility of being black you couldn't deny

so, you denied my equality for your superiority

my hair

my skin

my lip

my nose

you made me believe straight hair is better

my hair is too wooly, wavy or kinky

you are blind to the beauty of my locks and braids

you don't understand it, so you try to question me

how dare you!

sorry, i do not have to explain my hue to you

i come in shades of the crust of the earth

you made fun of me, but does it make you feel better?

black is the color of my love

and it can never be black enough

my hair

my skin

my lip

my nose

i don't need your words to know my worth
neither do i need your love to heal my past
i'm not going to change any of this to suit you
i'm going to carry myself like the royal that i am
your words won't glue me down
and i will not be shaded out of my history
i'm black, i'm bold, i'm beautiful
i'm strong, i don't crack, and i'm standing tall
after all the havoc you have caused
striking like thunder with the sound of my voice
and i am the rainbow colors that shine after the rain
on my mighty feet, gallantly posing
this is who i am
and you will see me

my hair
my skin
my lip
my nose.

choke your lover

choke your lover while you kiss me
send him to hell for a night in my heaven
he loves you the most, but you want me more
give in to the lust i offer or be forever consecrated
while you wonder in his space, incarcerated.

immigration

to be me
to be free
just like the summer breeze

like a tree
blessed with fruits
i want to feed the world with mine

even though it comes with a toll
rather die paying for my expensive freedom
than to live, caged and afraid to show my colors

like a little bird
out of cage, learning to be me
if i fall on the way, i'd know i tried

one hit wonder

he rolled in like music

and left like a storm

i thought i could control it

but my emotions orchestrated my anger

not an angel

he said i'm like a rose
and i told him
remember roses do wither
and they also have thorns.

fallow

what is there to write about my sad life?
empty vast land of a painful memory
without edible fruits, but unfamiliar weed
these fruits could be poison to my soul
these weeds could be healing to my spirit
stationed with a monotonous surface
dig deeper, it's still as dry as the desert
even the weeds don't grow here anymore
neither do i want another day in this body

conversation with self

my outside visited my inside

they realized how different they both are

yet trapped in this little body of mine

without a fight,

they both agreed

my inside stays hidden reinforcing my outside

while my outside stays seen, protecting my inside

don't let them in

don't let them know

says my inside

won't let them in

won't let them know

unless they are worth it says my outside

i will draw them close but won't let them see you.

little fires

little fires everywhere,
coming together like lava
feel the heat, inhale the smoke
pompeii in america

like a fruit

he said—a little riper, i will be sweeter
we both know a little riper, i will start to rot

choices

eat it up and let it digest

or

you let it eat you up and be digested.

my mask

i knew i was different from the other boys
even though i didn't play with my sister's doll
i wanted something larger than the life ahead
daddy always made me sit to watch soccer
i swear to god i never understood it at all
i enjoyed the kitchen time with my mom
cooking some spicy yoruba soup while
we gossiped about my father and his anger
she talked about how the boys whistled when she walked the streets
i wished to tell her how i wanted to be chased by boys too
everyone picked on my love for shorts and birthday suit
i have been countlessly harassed for crossing my legs
why did my day get harder when i chose pink?
daddy's anger got triggered when i chose romance over action
harlequin was my favorite and hadley chase was his
writing was the only way to voice my truth
other than my black jacket that hid my porno-magazines
always elated when i naomi-campbell-walked in my mother's stilettoes
even with my femininity, i am still a man
in my one world with two separate souls

my personality split depends on who i am with

i don't know how i found the strength to carry these spirits

but i did a great job hiding for a while

before my happiness started tearing down the mask

when is love enough?

when is love enough?
the day you bit me with words
or the night you hit me first
when you lied your way to part my thighs
or when you could not swallow your huge pride

when is love enough?
when you dried me up like beef jerky?
or filled me up with your bitter tsunami?
when you blacked me out with your blindfold?
or when you painted your white lies with gold?

when is love truly enough?

the whisperer

the whisperer in the middle of the night
whenever i heard his whispers
someone went missing
someone's innocence diminished
i laid in bed wondering when my turn would be
no one believed the tales, nowhere to run
tick tock! the gentle breeze of evil
conjuring the whisperer to my cradle
i shut my eyes, but heaven was far away
shhhhhhh! that was his voice
he rumbled in my ear "don't say a word or you will die"
the big hand that was meant to protect me slipped into my nicker
i closed my eyes scared to see what his face looked like at that time
he was a monster, a blood sucker, i begged him to stop
but he touched me
he touched me in every sensitive place, and i hated myself
and then, i hated that i enjoyed what he did to me
i found pleasure in this pain and i felt insane
i lost to him my beautiful pride, unsure i ever had any
he left like the wind while i was rolling in my thoughts

i laid in the pool of my own blood wondering

why didn't i scream?

neither of us ever screamed

the whisperer will come for you again if he enjoyed it

why were they so sure about this?

i prayed he wouldn't, but would that have meant my body wasn't good enough

my teenage brain couldn't process much

but i just wanted to be enough, enough for him to come again

no one believed my story about the whisperer

it was only a dream, and i buried the hurt in my dream pot

traveler

long winter days
obscure with haze
short lonely night
sleeping is a fight

elves and evil fay
trip me round the bay
as i follow in fright
they say i'll be fine

grateful

the sky has a heart
when it breaks
then it rains
and eases my pain

some stars are not bright
but with their dim lights
they beautify the sky
and perfect my night

in hand, maybe little
but tomorrow is a mystery
with deep gratitude
i shoot for a great altitude

someone else

i want you
you want someone else
i love you
someone else is your love
i wish i was someone else
while someone else was me

i make you smile
but someone else makes you cry
i'm always by your side
when someone else is nowhere to be found
still, all you long for is someone else
can't i just be someone else?

you say i'm your best friend
and someone else is your soulmate
someone else should be your best friend
and i your soulmate
i am exhausted from being myself
maybe if i'm someone else, just maybe!

crazy nancy

i'm not a big listener of new songs
cause i think the old songs sound better
i'm not an eater of junk
cause i want to stay slim and cancer free
my mother said it's all in my head.

i'm grateful when the sun is shining
why shouldn't everyone be happy?
i'm praying my neighbor will stop crying
cause her husband left her for crazy nancy
my father says it's not my business.

jẹ-jẹ

every day inside lagos city
i see people with hard faces
going to different workplaces
sad, sober and somber
can they just take it slow?

every day seems the same
everyone looking for a change
mentally and spiritually caged
wishing, hoping and praying
can they just let it go?

every day with a big task
who is ready to pay the price?
young boys looking for fast track
beautiful girls digging for naira
suffering, smiling and pretending
can they just breathe in slow?

look at you now

rooted in hell
branches of disaster
flowers of deception
that's the tree you've become

fruits of death
soiled in revenge
a standing monster
that's what you've become

you can blind their eyes
corrupt their minds
i'm not moved by your lies
i know what you've become

you're as dark as the night
you're sad and wild
you can pretend to them
but this is who you have become

different world

you've got the love
but i never get enough
you've got it all
but i never had it once

you enjoy every bit of life
but i suffer every day of mine
you have nothing to regret
but i have nothing to live for

you think we are all the same
but i know we are far from same
you're the high, rich and mighty
but i'm the low, poor and filthy.

covalent bond

i don't know what is good for me
but right now, you look so good on me
just like crystal jellyfish in the sea
you make me glow softly

i don't know what i'm feeling
but i love how it makes me feel
high on something far from drugs
addicted to your kind of love

i'm not looking for a remedy to your spell
i love myself in your scenic shackles
i don't want to be free
it's a bond i'm not willing to break

our foolish pride

we are both too tired to sleep
we are both to careless to keep
we are both too proud to weep
we are both too good to be

we are both too shy to hit
we are both too lazy to dig
we are both too perfect to fit
that's why we never go deep

our pride is our foolish ride
never wrong but always right
our greed puts us in a fight
and we fall on different sides

obsession

glued to my heart
always in my head
in my dreams every night
it's like you're next to my bed

forgetting you is impossible
a war in my mind and soul
your disease is incurable
you've left my body totally cold

waiting for death to end your game
but every day seems to be a rematch
you have me completely tamed
it is hard to be your only desire

priceless immortality

made of clay
so, they say
live every day
like you'll die today

dust to dust
the unbreakable curse
death ends the strain
but what do i have to gain?

priceless immortality
made us all a casualty
i fulfil the food chain
when i am buried to decay

bleeding rose

took the pain and made it look good
it's so real but you won't believe it
all the tears and injuries are hidden
that's how the rose bleeds

blooming with colors of wretchedness
looks expensive even though it's dirty
like a gift with an obscure curse
the way the rose bleeds

they don't know on the inside
she's abused and underrated
she tries to prove she's a good girl
exactly when the rose bleeds

my guidance

he thought he could guide me
when he can't see his own back
he walked away leaving things undone
on my own, i got it all done

he's too focused to realize what he missed
i was too young to make him understand and see
he's my father, he's supposed to know better
i am his son, and i don't want to go wrong

filthy and guilty

my pathetic confusion is the reason for my self-lies
my delusion is the reason why i think you and i will someday fly
even though my tears over you never run dry
i still convince myself you are the reason why i'm alive

in your court of love, i am found guilty
my undying love for you is the reason i am filthy
how did i spend so much time with you?
i just want to let go and live without you

unprotected sex

up-high cloud
down-low ground
horny young folks
satisfying their kicking hormones
on a moving school bus

sad long days
snail-slow pace
lucky sad man
drink cold beer
after a great quick sex

bright blue sky
summer sunshine
on a moving school bus
after a great quick sex
comes her first unwanted child

ready to be taken

you filled me with an undeniable desire

an act of an unquestionable sire

i know you hide inside you a big fire

the flame in your eyes like sapphire

tells me you're a sweet liar

you're a soft pretender

like an unpredictable weather

you're a beautiful story tellee

where your imaginations are from, i wonder

you're so good and you photograph it better

after everything you're so tender

i'm convinced you're a great kisser

but you never ask, will you ever?

you're so tough and pretty clever

just don't be a time loafer

i can't breathe

i can't breathe
even when oxygen is free
i can't live
because my blackness threatens your kind
me on the ground
gun in your hand
and yet you are scared
of what?

you are threatened because i aspire
to inspire my kin and clans
after all your plans to hold down my race
enslaved and segregated, yet my kind ruled
why do you have so much hatred for me?
just why?

american soil and flag
soaked in the blood and cry
of black men and women
taken in their prime

as guns and bullets continue to depopulate my race

travelling in the sound of american breeze

the fainting voice of a black child

chanting i can't breathe

now he can't breathe

should you live in peace?

my dog and i

in my high-rise new york building
when the siren blows, my dog howls
i washed my hands with soap
and sprayed surfaces with lysol.
this is new to us — just like the virus
neither my dog nor i usually care about the "where-where" sound
police on the move or just an ambulance trying to get through

i look through my window, it's an empty street
i turn on the tv, death rate is increasing
this alarm goes off every minute
and someone, somewhere is gasping for air
"do your part to flatten the curve"
i lay in bed not sure if i should say a prayer
or question the great and almighty
why?

Words in My Head

Ayodeji Otuyelu

coalescing was how we used to survive
but there is power in staying away from one another
undaunted to tell my father how alcohol helped me cope
he is fine to hear that, as long i stay at home
friendly meetings are totally unacceptable
i run at the sight of a weak looking neighbor
we are all locked in the prison of our home

i doubt i remember what being social really means
peace to all the people who have lost their dear ones
solace in the quality of air in india
hope in the dolphins found in venice
forgive us merciful lord
and grant our desire to be wild and free again

hunting

seven years into the world unknown

it was a day before my birthday

looking at my mother putting on make up

she watched me watch her through the mirror

come closer baby she said

and she put the red lipstick on me

she laughed out loud and whispered

you have lips just like mine

i asked if i could wear the eyebrow-pencil

she handed it over

i had tried my writing pencil on my brows many times

with my little hand i drew an un-arched line

she watched and laughed

took the pencil and corrected the line

she looked straight into my eyes and smiled

don't let your father see it she mumbled

you are my beautiful boy

she wiped my face singing "my beautiful child"

she wished so badly for a female child,

but my father boasted of strong genes

gently my father prepared me for hunting
i never liked guns nor the woods
i was afraid of being hunted in my dreams
by the spirits of dead animals
but i love the mirror, the colors and my reflection
i love the gowns, the jewelry and the shoes
don't fall my mother exclaimed
whenever i wore her oversized pumps
her white wedding heels were my favorite
pointy, sharp, three inch stilettoes
we had just finished my make-up and
i was wearing my mother's highest heels
when the door flung open

my father walked in
he never knocked!
he just entered like a thief
the disgust on his face, the fear on my face
the sorry face my mother wore like make-up
clarified my mother's warnings
he screamed at her and dragged me to the bathroom
i saw dark tears in the bathroom mirror

reminding me of the broken-hearted beauty on tv
he scrubbed my face hard i thought my skin would peel
don't turn my son into a girl! he is a man
that was the last time my mother allowed me to be me
that day created a silence between her and i
and increased the pressure from him

i was sure i would shoot myself one day while hunting
but i did not! neither did i ever shoot an antelope
finally, one day while hunting i pulled the trigger
and left father's blood on the ground
but unsure why i was bleeding from my arms

everything in between

between my truth and lies
between my love and madness
between my secret and openness
between my peace and sadness
i found you
right between my heaven and hell
dwelling between my road and home
still between my pleasure and guilt
i found you

Extra; From my next book

a woman's religion

this ritual was my drug
prescribed by him — my lord
he owns me, he knows me
he and he alone have the authority.
he slaps me when i make mistakes
he punches me when i disobey
i asked my mother if there was a way
she told me "she worshipped in this same church"
the only way is to cling to my prayers and songs
and obey the statutes created by him and his kind
my father, my grandfather and great grandfather
this is our religion, this is our faith
he provided me with poison, and i swallowed
my tears turn him on, and he gets excited
i dare not say no!
with the pain in my stomach
and my teary eyes, i received my messiah
he forced his hoe into my dry land

        and began to speak in tongues while he thrust
he dug and dug deep, until he busted his water in my well
then blamed my inability to conceive on my stubbornness
you are a woman — be one
be fruitful, let your stomach hold my seeds
don't think and don't try to be
misconception of his love for me because of the money he makes

i could have done better had i been given a chance
i watched him boast among his friends of his riches and trophy wife
and he expected me to be gleeful among my friends
because of the jewelries and clothes, he gave me
that should be my pride as a woman
this is not the life i dreamt of in my sleep
but my mother told me dreams are the ways the devil misleads us

i ate my silence and finally pushed out my daughter
sharp mouthed, with the smooth voice i lost
she spoke and her father froze still
i knew my strength was preserved to protect her
her head up high like an egyptian obelisk
in the wind of men, she danced to the rhythm
she challenged the warrior to a sword fight
and yet she put on her make-up and danced by the riverside
she was my revenge; she was his plague.

Glossary

Maami: *mother*

Mama Agba: *grand mother*

Iroko Oluwere: *Iroko is a large hardwood tree from the west coast of tropical Africa that can live up to 500 years. Yoruba's believed to have supernatural properties.*

Wahala: *problems*

Kokoro: *a rod-like shaped crunchy Nigerian snack made with corn meal and spices.*

Ogogoro: *alcohol*

Jeje: *slow down*

Naira: the currency of Nigeria.

A special thanks to all those people
who got on the rollercoaster with me,
knowing it's going to be rough, and yet made it fun.

Maya Angelou's poetry taught me
how to celebrate my skin color

Lana Del Rey songs has always been part of my inspiration

To my Uncle Wale thank you for always being supportive

To my friend 6th thank you for being an art to me

The list goes on but thank you all...

ABOUT THE AUTHOR

Ayodeji Otuyelu was born in Ogun State, Nigeria, but currently resides in New York City. At a young age, he started writing poems as an outlet for his overwhelming emotions but kept them a secret in his diary. It wasn't until he started hosting Open Mics at Tsion Café, an Ethiopian restaurant in Harlem, that he found the confidence to share his writings and thoughts with the public. These writings were mostly centered around his experiences living in both Nigeria and the United States. His first publication *Words in My Head*, explores a variety of themes ranging from love, sex, sadness, and the overall complexities of life. When he is not writing, he enjoys modeling as another form of expression and celebration of the African body through implied nudes and portraits. His poem *Ungodly Feeling was* featured in the online poetry blog Bluepepper.

Twitter : @coolejjy
Instagram : @coolejjy
Email : info@ayodejiotuyelu.com
Website : www.ayodejiotuyelu.com

www.ingramcontent.com/pod-product-compliance
Lightning Source LLC
Chambersburg PA
CBHW022111090426
42743CB00008B/807